Next Time You See a
PILL BUG

BY EMILY MORGAN

NSTA **Kids**
National Science Teachers Association
Arlington, Virginia

National Science Teachers Association

Claire Reinburg, Director
Wendy Rubin, Managing Editor
Andrew Cooke, Senior Editor
Amanda O'Brien, Associate Editor
Amy America, Book Acquisitions Coordinator

ART AND DESIGN
Will Thomas Jr., Director

PRINTING AND PRODUCTION
Catherine Lorrain, Director

NATIONAL SCIENCE TEACHERS ASSOCIATION
David L. Evans, Executive Director
David Beacom, Publisher

1840 Wilson Blvd., Arlington, VA 22201
www.nsta.org/store
For customer service inquiries, please call 800-277-5300.

Lexile® measure: 640L

Special thanks to Don Salvatore, science educator at the Boston Museum of Science, and Dr. Keith Summerville, associate professor of environmental science and associate dean at the College of Arts and Sciences at Drake University, for reviewing this manuscript.

Library of Congress Cataloging-in-Publication Data
Morgan, Emily, author.
  Next time you see a pill bug / by Emily Morgan.
      pages cm. -- (Next time you see)
   Summary: "Chances are that just under a nearby rock, you'll spot a roly-poly pill bug. Encourage a child to take a close look, and introduce a fascinating creature. Gently pick it up and watch as it rolls into a ball and unrolls to take a walk. This cousin to lobsters and crabs sheds its crusty skin and will tickle your hand with its 14 (count 'em!) wiggly legs. The book will inspire elementary-age children to experience the enchantment of everyday phenomena such as pill bugs"-- Provided by publisher.
  Audience: Grade K to 3.
   ISBN 978-1-936959-17-4 -- ISBN 978-1-938946-17-2 (library binding) -- ISBN 978-1-938946-78-3 (e-book)
 1. Wood lice (Crustaceans)--Juvenile literature. I. Title.
  QL444.M34M67 2013
  595.3'72--dc23
                    2013035270

Cataloging-in-Publication Data are also available from the Library of Congress for the e-book.
e-LCCN: 2013035719

For Jack, who likes to collect "roly-polies"

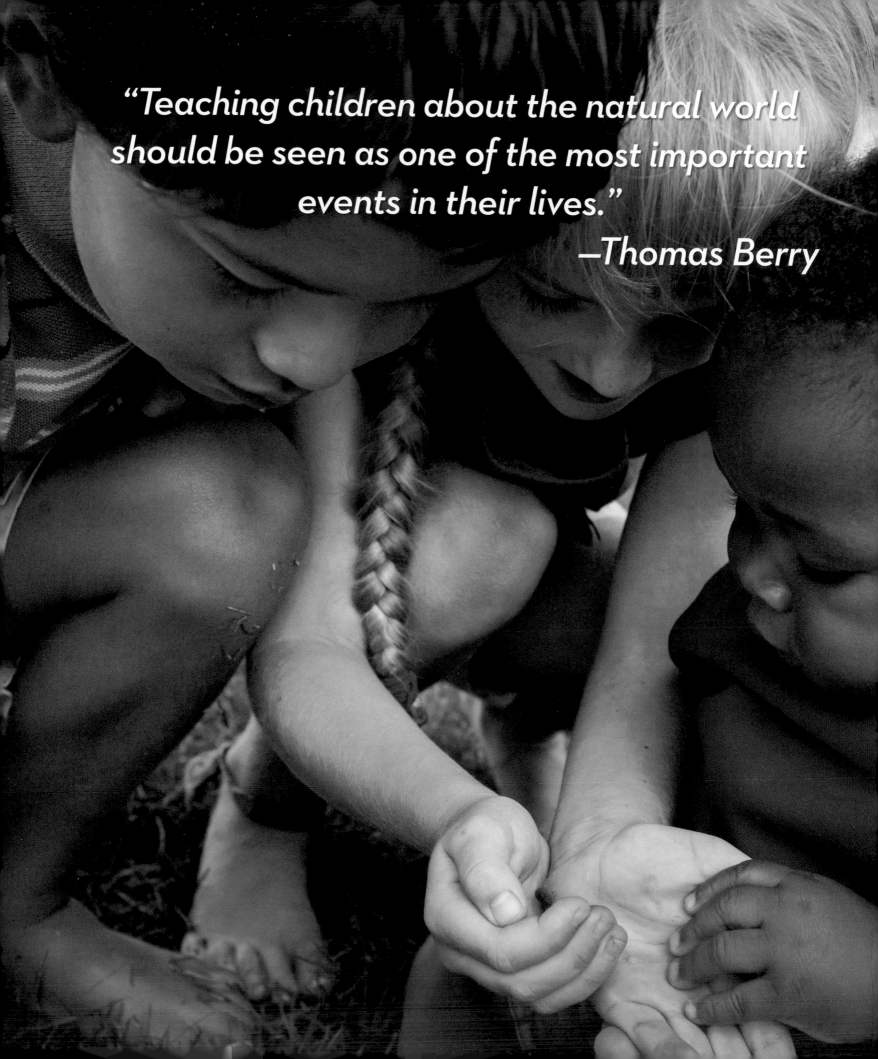

"Teaching children about the natural world should be seen as one of the most important events in their lives."

—Thomas Berry

A Note to Parents and Teachers

The books in this series are intended to be read with a child *after* he has had some experience with the featured objects or phenomena. For example, turn over some stones or logs in your yard or nearby park and collect a few pill bugs. Watch them roll up in a ball when touched. Let them open up and crawl around in your hands; they won't bite! Place a few in a jar or bug box and try to count their wiggling legs. Discuss what you observe and what you wonder about these little animals. What do they eat? Why do they live under rocks and logs? Do they lay eggs?

Then, after placing the pill bugs gently back where you got them or in a container nearby, read this book together. Take time to pause and share your learnings and wonderings with each other. You will find that new learnings often lead to more questions.

These books are not meant to present facts to be memorized. They are meant to inspire a sense of wonder about ordinary objects or phenomena and foster a desire to learn more about the natural world. Pill bugs are fairly common animals, but when you stop to think about the fact that they are crustaceans and not bugs at all, and that they are closely related to shrimp and crabs that live in the sea, they become so much more remarkable. My wish is that after reading this book, you and your child feel a sense of wonder the next time you see a pill bug.

—Emily Morgan

Next time you see a pill bug, gently pick it up and hold it in your hand. Does it roll up into a ball? If so, be still and wait a few seconds for it to unroll. Let it crawl around. Look closely. What shape is it? What color is it? Can you count its legs? Does it have eyes, a mouth, a nose, or ears? What words can you use to describe it? How does your hand feel as the pill bug moves around?

Some people call these animals "roly-polies" because they roll up into balls when they are touched. Others call them pill bugs because their bodies are shaped like pills. But these creatures are not really bugs at all. They are not even insects.

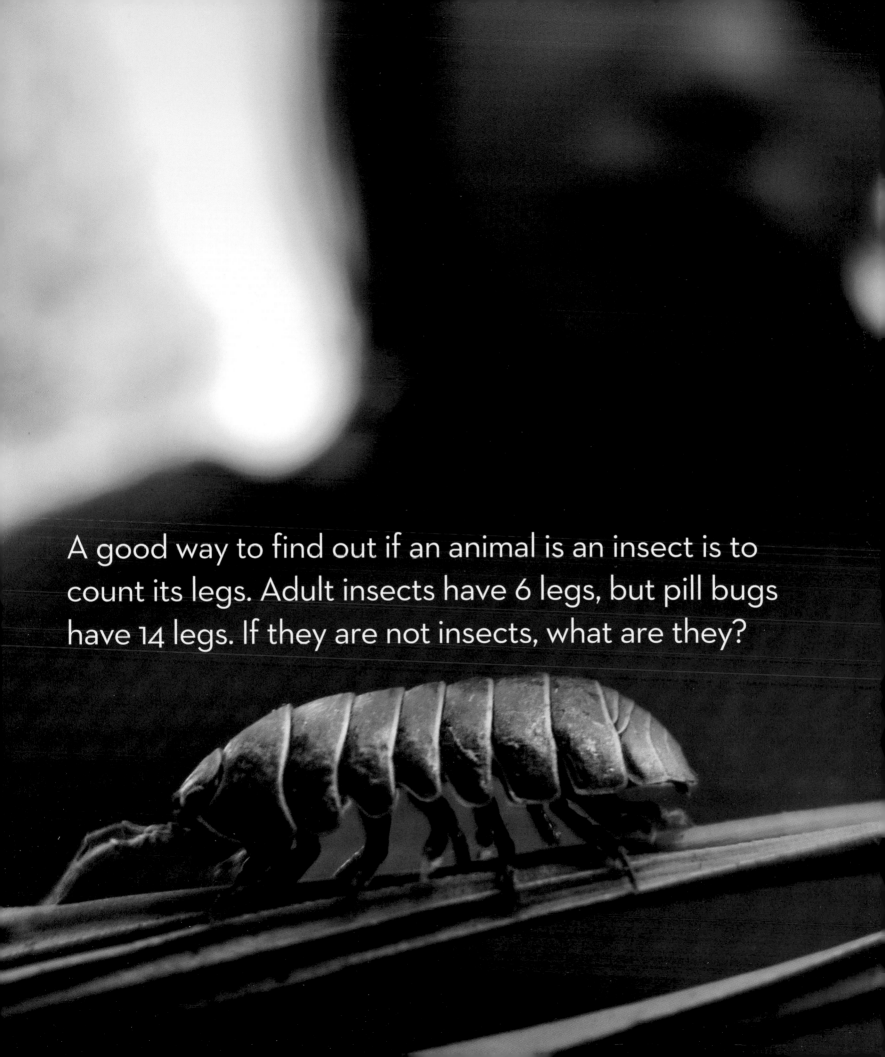

A good way to find out if an animal is an insect is to count its legs. Adult insects have 6 legs, but pill bugs have 14 legs. If they are not insects, what are they?

Crustaceans! When most people hear the word **crustacean**, they think of crabs, lobsters, and shrimp. It's true that most crustaceans live in or near the ocean, but pill bugs are unusual crustaceans. They live their entire lives on land.

Like all crustaceans, pill bugs hatch from eggs. A female pill bug carries her eggs underneath her body. After the eggs hatch, she carries her tiny babies in a pouch for a few days or weeks. Baby pill bugs look a lot like their parents, but they are much smaller and lighter in color.

Crustaceans have exoskeletons, or hard outer coverings. A pill bug's exoskeleton is thick on the top of its body and thinner on its underside, where the legs are attached.

One of the most interesting things about a pill bug is how it uses its exoskeleton to defend itself. When a pill bug is threatened, it rolls up into a ball. This way, the exoskeleton protects the inner, softer part of its body.

When you look closely at a pill bug, you notice that its exoskeleton is segmented, or divided into sections. All crustaceans are segmented. Another thing crustaceans have in common is that their exoskeletons do not grow as the rest of their bodies grow. So pill bugs must grow a new exoskeleton and shed the old one. This is called molting. They do this in two parts. First, they shed the back half, and a few days later, they shed the front half. If you see a pill bug that looks brownish-red on half of its body, it's probably molting.

Most crustaceans—such as crabs, lobsters, and crayfish—have claws or pinchers on some of their feet. However, pill bugs are different. All of their feet look the same. Because of this difference, scientists call pill bugs *isopods*, which means "same feet."

Compare the pill bug to the other crustaceans on these pages. What similarities and differences do you notice?

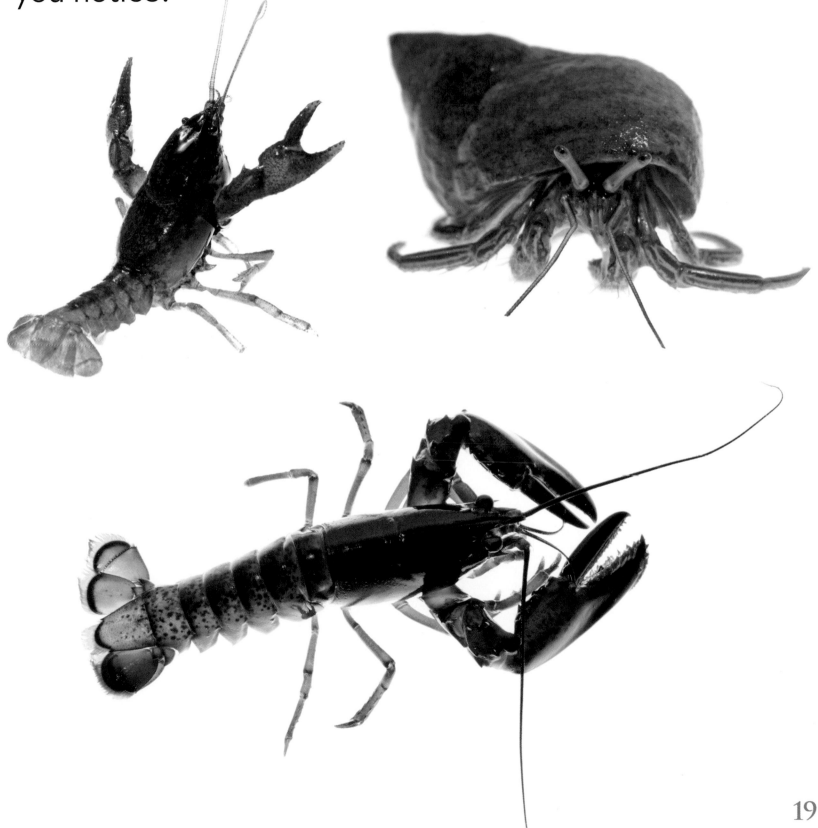

There is another kind of isopod that looks very similar to a pill bug. It is called a sow bug.

To tell the difference between these two isopods, look closely at the shapes of their bodies. A sow bug's body is flatter on the edges than a pill bug's body, and it has two points sticking out of its last segment. Also, a sow bug is not able to roll itself into a tight ball like a pill bug.

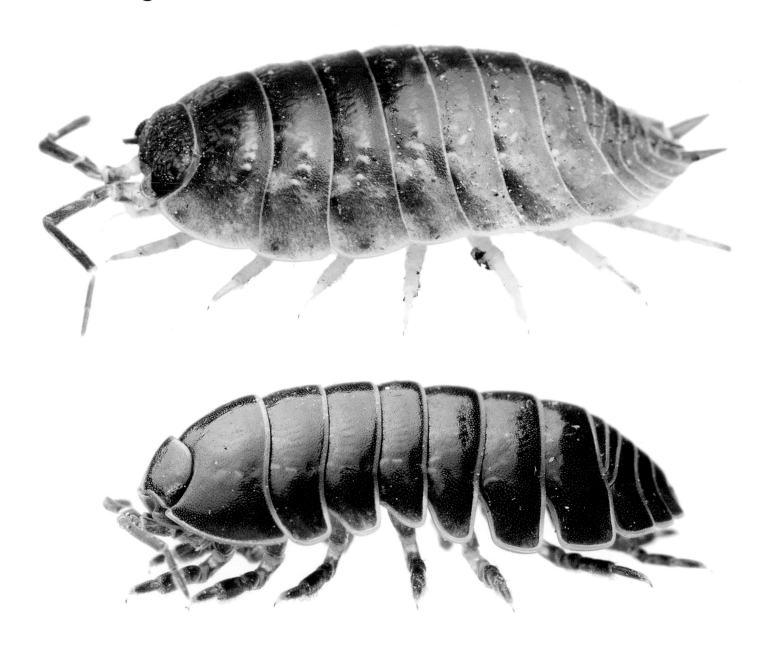

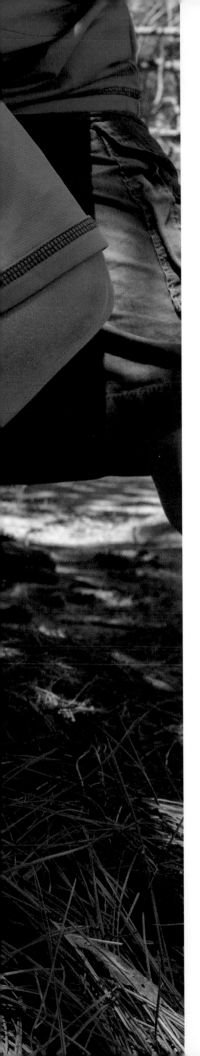

Pill bugs can live in many different places as long as they can find rotting plants, or sometimes the shoots of new plants, to eat. They also need moisture and seem to prefer dark places. If you are searching for pill bugs, a good place to check is under a log or stone. Have you ever wondered how pill bugs breathe under there?

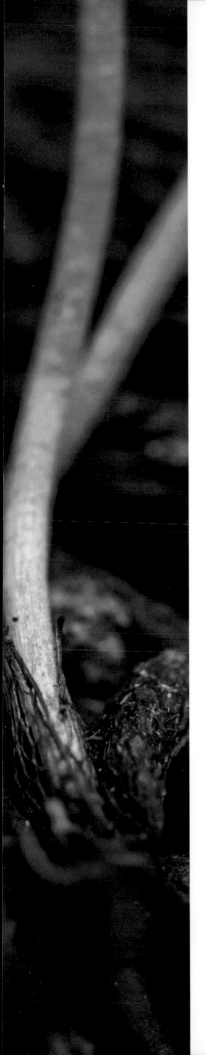

Like most crustaceans, pill bugs breathe through gills. Their gills must be moist for them to breathe. That's why the damp environment under rocks and logs is a great place for pill bugs to live. Unlike most other crustaceans, pill bugs cannot survive under water for a long period of time. So a place that is damp, but not too wet, is the perfect place for a pill bug to live.

Pill bugs are fun to watch and they don't bite. If you want to collect some pill bugs to observe, place them gently in a container. If you are going to keep them for more than a few minutes, add a damp paper towel so they don't dry out. After you observe them, be sure to put them back where you found them.